Jim Arnosky

Tooth & Claw

THE WILD WORLD OF BIG PREDATORS

STERLING CHILDREN'S BOOKS
New York

For Barbara Lalicki

STERLING CHILDREN'S BOOKS
New York

An Imprint of Sterling Publishing
387 Park Avenue South
New York, NY 10016

STERLING CHILDREN'S BOOKS and the distinctive Sterling Children's Books logo are trademarks of Sterling Publishing Co., Inc.

Display lettering created by Paul Shaw
Design by Andrea Miller
The artwork for this book was prepared using pencil and acrylic paints.

ISBN 978-1-4027-8624-2

Library of Congress Cataloging-in-Publication Data

Arnosky, Jim, author.
  Tooth and claw : the wild world of big predators / Jim Arnosky.
    pages cm
  Audience: Ages 6-10.
  Audience: Grades K to 3.
  ISBN 978-1-4027-8624-2
  1. Carnivora--Juvenile literature. 2. Predatory animals--Juvenile literature. I. Title.
  QL737.C2A76 2014
  599.7--dc23
                              2013033794

Distributed in Canada by Sterling Publishing
c/o Canadian Manda Group, 165 Dufferin Street
Toronto, Ontario, Canada M6K 3H6
Distributed in the United Kingdom by GMC Distribution Services
Castle Place, 166 High Street, Lewes, East Sussex, England BN7 1XU
Distributed in Australia by Capricorn Link (Australia) Pty. Ltd.
P.O. Box 704, Windsor, NSW 2756, Australia

For information about custom editions, special sales, and premium and corporate purchases, please contact Sterling Special Sales at 800-805-5489 or specialsales@sterlingpublishing.com.

Manufactured in China
Lot #:
2   4   6   8   10   9   7   5   3   1
01/14

www.sterlingpublishing.com/kids

CONTENTS

FOLD OUT!

FOLD OUT!

FOLD OUT!

FOLD OUT!

BENGAL TIGER

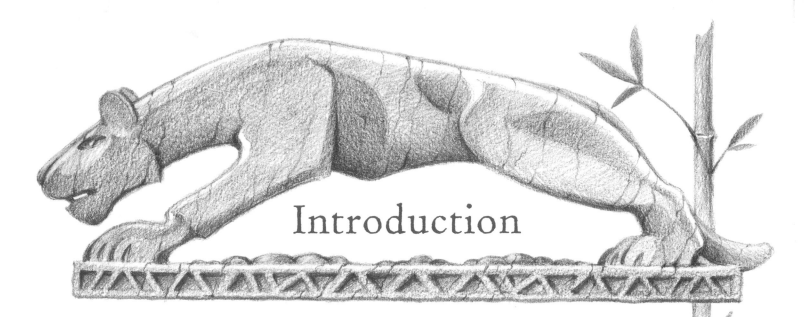

Introduction

I met a man from Pakistan, a country in Asia, who came face to face with a tiger one day when he was a small boy. He was walking along the edge of a field when a tiger suddenly stepped out of the tall grass and stood in front of him. The man said that he was certain the tiger was going to eat him. But the tiger did not attack. Instead, it lay down and let the boy pass. To this day, the storyteller feels that the good luck of that moment has stayed with him.

Good luck, indeed! An adult tiger can be almost twelve feet long from nose to tail tip and can weigh over 500 pounds. It can kill a bull by biting into and snapping its neck with one powerful, wrenching twist.

Wild tigers once ranged all across Asia. But due almost entirely to over-hunting, they have become scarce, and in some Asian countries, extinct. Yet these magnificent beasts continue to inhabit the jungles of our imagination. Deep down, we know that their very existence someplace, somewhere, somehow enhances our own lives. Even though there are more tigers today in zoos than those living in the wild, we think of them as only wild, always wild, forever wild.

This book is about the big wild cats of the world and some other large and awe-inspiring carnivores. Follow their huge paw prints with me. Let's learn more about the great carnivores who live their lives by tooth and claw.

Jim Arnosky

AFRICAN LION

African Lion

I grew up thinking that lions and tigers lived together in the jungles of Africa. This is how I saw them on TV and in movies. But in truth the only place a lion might see a tiger is in a zoo. In the wild, tigers are found on the Asian continent. Lions once lived in Asia, Europe, and Africa. And before the ice age that ended over 10,000 years ago, lions as big as the ones living in Africa roamed North America. Today, there are still some Asian lions, but almost all lions are native to Africa, where they live and hunt on the broad grasslands called savannas.

Second only to the tiger in size, African lions grow to be ten feet long and weigh over 500 pounds. Picture a cat very much like the one lounging on your couch—except it's longer than the couch and weighs three times as much!

Like most cats, large or small, lions have four toes on each hind foot and five on each front foot. The fifth toe comes into play only when climbing, fighting, or catching prey. Being higher on the leg, the cat's fifth toe does not register in footprints. Neither do the claws, which are retractable and are usually not extended while a cat walks or runs. Cat claws do not actually bend or fold to retract. It is the toes that retract by curling up inside the paw, much the way you sometimes curl up your fingers inside your mitten.

Left front foot showing retractable claws.

African Lion track

4½"

claws "unsheathed"

Because retractable claws do not wear down from constant contact with the ground, they stay sharp for clawing prey.

Interlocking teeth

All land carnivores have interlocking teeth that shear meat and provide a vise-like grip on their prey. With the combination of interlocking teeth and massive jawbones, a lion clamps down with such terrific force it can crush veins, tendons, and muscles, and break big bones.

African Lion skull

A PRIDE OF LIONS

The African lion is truly the king of the beasts. With no natural enemy, lions live fearlessly, out in the open. Only when stalking prey do lions become furtive and hide, taking advantage of their tan coloration that blends into the golden grasses of the savanna.

African lions live in groups called prides. There can be as few as four and as many as twenty lions in a pride. Only the males grow manes, which are thick mats of hair surrounding the head and covering the neck. Dominance among the males in the pride is attained by size and maintained by ferocious fighting ability.

A female lion, called a lioness, is smaller than a male but a more deadly hunter. In fact, the entire pride is kept fed mostly by the hunting skills of the females. Lionesses hunt in groups, stalking and surrounding their prey before chasing it at speeds upwards of thirty-five miles per hour. One female will leap on the back of a fleeing zebra, gazelle, buffalo, or even an elephant, dig her claws into the skin, and hang on, dragging, until the other lions catch up and do the same. Eventually the combined weight of lions pulls the prey to the ground, and a bite to the throat ends the struggle. The animals killed are usually young or old and very weak.

Lions hunt both day and night, depending on when they had their last meal and have become hungry again. They can't wait too long between hunts because it takes a tremendous amount of energy to run down fleet-footed prey.

A pride is usually led by the largest male. Sometimes two or more males, often brothers, will lead the pride together.

AFRICAN LEOPARD

African Leopard

The African leopard is the smallest of the big cats. A large male African leopard is 125 pounds of sudden, blurring action and lightning-fast claws.

Leopards are solitary animals. Only during breeding season, or when a mother is with her kittens, are leopards seen together. These beautiful creatures are largely nocturnal, resting during daylight hours high up in the limbs of trees. They do their hunting from dusk to dawn, padding silently on large paws, moving stealthily as they slowly stalk their prey.

A leopard attacks by biting and clawing and is capable of killing an animal twice its size. Most of a leopard's diet consists of small antelopes, which the big cat can carry in its mouth as it climbs a tree to a high branch. There the leopard can eat, safe away from hyenas and other hungry predators that would steal food.

Friends of mine who work with wildlife in Africa have told me that the leopard's fur, with its tight rings of spots called rosettes, blends with almost any background. I found this hard to believe, considering how eye-catching the rosettes are. Then I painted this leopard and with each new rosette I added, the more my leopard seemed to recede into the scene. I could see how the leopard's rosettes of spots visually break up the animal's light-colored fur. And the result makes the big cat practically disappear before your eyes.

Jaguar

Leopard

Cheetah

The three largest spotted cats have distinctly different spot patterns.

Cheetah

CHEETAH

A full-grown cheetah weighs 120 pounds and is about seven feet long from nose to the tip of its tail. Cheetahs live in Africa's open plains, where dark green trees dot the landscape. But you will not find them hiding in the shadows of trees as leopards do. Cheetahs roam freely and boldly in broad daylight, as if they know they can outrun any danger. Because of its visibility, the cheetah is one of the most observed big cats, even though cheetah numbers are dwindling.

The cheetah is the only big cat that does not have retractable claws. Always exposed, cheetah claws become worn and dull from constant scraping on the ground. They are not used for catching and killing prey the way all other cat claws are. More like the toenails of a dog or wolf, cheetah claws are used primarily for traction when running.

Cheetahs are canine-like in other ways, too. A cheetah has the long, flexible back and tall, thin legs of a greyhound. Cheetahs make a very doggy sounding bark. And like canines, cheetahs chase a fleeing animal, crowding and tripping its legs to make it fall.

The cheetah is the fastest land animal on the planet. Reaching a speed of over seventy miles per hour, a cheetah can run down the speediest antelope in a matter of seconds. Cheetahs are made for the chase with strong, long springy legs, toenails that dig in with each running step, and an extra-long tail to provide balance when turning abruptly to keep pace with frantic zig-zagging prey.

With all its speed and grace while running, to my mind, a cheetah is most beautiful to look upon when it is lying in repose—intelligent, alert, always ready to run.

AMERICAN LION

American Lion

The American lion, more commonly known as the mountain lion, cougar, panther, or puma, can be found in North, Central, and South America. Their uniformly tan coloration makes them virtually invisible in all of their habitats, which include forests, swamps, canyon lands, and deserts. They are secretive, solitary, sneaky, mostly nocturnal, and rarely seen, even where they are numerous.

Mountain lions grow to be seven to nine feet long including the tail, and weigh as much as 200 pounds. These big cats feed primarily on deer, which they catch by jumping down on them from above, or stalking close enough to chase. They also kill and eat birds, beavers, rabbits, raccoons, and coyotes.

In my home state of Vermont, the original big cat of the mountains, known as the "catamount," became extinct early in the twentieth century. But since then, other mountain lions from the American West and Canadian East have found their way into the catamount's ancestral range. I have tracked a number of these "new" lions. One day I found prints in snow that showed where a big cat had leaped from the forest floor to the top of a boulder, seven feet high.

While in most places American lions are holding their own or making a comeback, the Florida panther (pictured above) remains rare and endangered.

The only American wildcat larger than the mountain lion is the jaguar. See these prints life-size on pages 30 and 31!

Jaguar

At eight feet in length and weighing over 300 pounds, the jaguar is the largest cat in the Western Hemisphere. Jaguars are spotted cats, similar to leopards but much larger. Jaguars are found in parts of Texas, Arizona, and New Mexico. But they are most common in Mexico, Central America, and South America. Jaguars that live in dry places eat peccaries (small wild pigs), deer, snakes, birds, and rabbits. Incredibly strong, a single jaguar can even kill a horse and drag it away.

Jungle jaguars climb trees to eat nesting birds. They also hunt near water for fish, caimans, crocodiles, and snakes, including anacondas, which are also large predators that occasionally eat jaguars.

The anaconda kills prey by coiling around and squeezing the life out of it before swallowing it whole. An anaconda is able to swallow prey as large as a jaguar because the snake's jaws are attached to the skull by stretchy ligaments and the chin is separated at the middle, allowing the mouth to widen vertically and horizontally. Jaguars can kill anacondas only by avoiding the snake's razor sharp teeth and constricting coils of its massive body. They claw the snake to wound and weaken it for the final pounce and skull-crushing bite. The name *jaguar* comes from a South American word that means "kills in a single bound."

Jaguar in desert habitat.

Most jaguars have spotted fur. Some are born solid black. These are called black panthers.

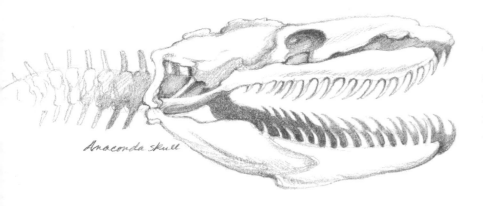

Anaconda skull

The green anaconda is a monster of a snake that can grow to be over thirty feet long and weigh 600 pounds, making it not only the longest but also the heaviest snake in the world.

GRIZZLY BEAR

At one time, the grizzly and brown bear were thought to be two separate species. Today it is believed they are the same species, with the brown bear being a larger version of the grizzly. Grizzly bears average four feet in height at the shoulders and seven feet long from nose to tail. Most weigh 600 pounds. But there are grizzlies that weigh well over 1,000 pounds! Their huge size and nasty temperament make grizzly bears the most dangerous of all land carnivores. They do not retreat or flee or slip away when encountered, as most wild animals do. They stand their ground and will attack. Stories of people being killed and eaten by grizzlies are true.

Grizzlies have an incredible sense of smell and can follow the scent of carrion (dead animal flesh) for many miles. They also kill and eat deer, elk, moose, rodents, rabbits, birds, fish—and anything else they can get their huge paws on. Besides meat, grizzlies gobble up nuts, berries, and grasses.

These massive animals move fast. A grizzly that seems a safe distance away can charge unprovoked, running forty miles per hour, and suddenly be dangerously close.

GRIZZLY BEAR

BLACK BEAR

Black Bear

The first wild bear I ever saw was a black bear that was standing on the edge of a beaver pond, eating tall grasses. Another time, I rushed outdoors with my sketch pad after being told that a black bear was fishing in our river. And it was yet another black bear that broke a limb of our neighbor's apple tree while climbing to feast on the ripened fruit. Grasses, fish, fruit, nuts, honey, berries, insects, birds, reptiles, and mammals all make up a black bear's diet. An animal that will eat almost anything is called an omnivore. All bears—black, brown, grizzly, and even polar bears—are omnivorous.

An omnivorous diet makes a bear grow large. Adult black bears average 350 pounds with a maximum weight of 700 pounds. Big bears travel slowly, waddling flat-footed from feeding area to feeding area. But even the biggest bear can move surprisingly fast when it charges or flees.

In cold climates, bears fatten up in autumn and live on that fat while sleeping in their winter dens. To sleep soundly, bears try to find den sites with a northern exposure that will stay cold until spring.

Black bears are found in the United States, Canada, and Mexico. In the United States, east of the Mississippi River, the only bear is the black bear. Throughout the West, however, black bears share their habitat with grizzlies and, in the Northwest, brown bears.

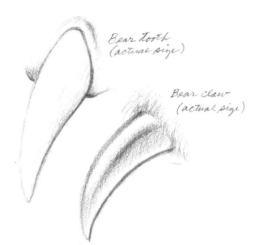

Bears crave protein-rich insects, which they claw out of rotted wood.

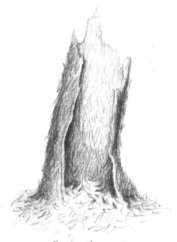

Rotted tree stumps hollowed out by a bear.

Bears can eat almost anything because they have the strong, bone-cracking jaws and sharp, shearing front teeth of a meat eater, as well as the flat-crowned, plant-crushing back teeth of a plant eater.

POLAR BEAR

Polar bears are semi-aquatic mammals that travel over the polar ice and swim in Arctic waterways. Feeding almost entirely on fatty seals, a polar bear can weigh 2,000 pounds, making it the world's largest carnivorous land animal.

Like most bears, polar bears have few natural enemies. They have little to fear but human hunters and killer whales that may attack them while they swim. The greatest threat to polar bears is the loss of their frozen habitat. As the polar ice cap melts, the huge white bears swim longer and farther in search of floating ice on which to walk, run, sleep, breed, and raise their young.

BROWN BEAR

Brown bears are super-sized grizzlies! A brown bear can weigh 1,500 pounds. On all fours, they are nine feet long, and standing up on their hind legs, they tower ten feet high. Brown bears live on the western coast of Alaska, where they share their range with grizzlies and black bears. When salmon swim upstream to spawn, brown, grizzly, and black bears congregate on the rivers and gorge themselves with fish.

GRAY WOLF

Gray Wolf

In the silent forest where wolves live, my wife, Deanna, and I watched a pool of muddy water, waiting anxiously for the sounds of the thirsty animals coming to drink. We heard breezes in the treetops. We heard falling leaves landing on the forest floor. We heard the sound of our own breath as we tried to be as quiet as possible. Then we heard the soft press of big paws, stepping very slowly down the hillside, invisible but unmistakable, coming toward the pool and us.

When I finally spotted a wolf, it was peeking out from behind a tree. I saw one wolf eye staring. From tree to tree, peek to peek, stare to stare, the big gray wolf cautiously but steadily made its way down to the pool and took a long drink. In the quiet, the lapping of its tongue in the water echoed loudly in the wilderness.

All canines, including your own family dog, are descended from the gray wolf, also known as the timber wolf. Adult male gray wolves are six feet long from nose to tail tip and weigh 150 pounds. Females are slightly smaller. Gray wolves are found all over the world. Most are gray in color, but they can also be brown, black, or white. The red wolf, considered a separate species, is smaller and has shorter hair.

wolf

Coyote

The coyote can be distinguished from a wolf by its much narrower snout and smaller nose.

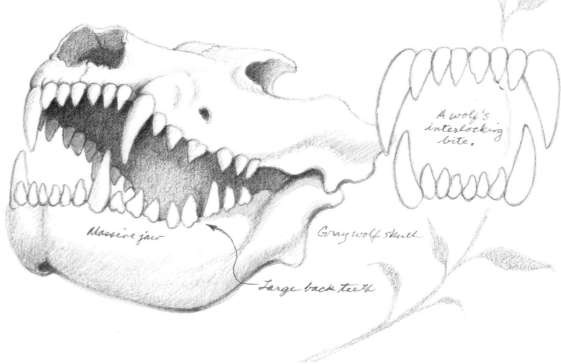

Wolf teeth are exceptionally large and every tooth is sharply pointed to cut and tear meat. A wolf's huge jaws are used for crushing bones.

Massive jaw

Large back teeth

Gray wolf skull

A wolf's interlocking bite.

WOLF PACKS

Wolves live in social groups called packs, made up of one or more wolf families. The pack is led by the largest and strongest (alpha) wolf and its mate. Only the alpha pair breed, but all the other wolves in the pack help care for the pups.

Hunting together, a pack of wolves can bring down deer, elk, caribou, moose, and even bison. The wolves chase and bite the running legs of large animals, causing them to fall. Then the wolves in the pack immediately begin to feed, even as their prey tries to free itself. Miraculously, many of the victims fight off the attack and get away. So the wolves must hunt continuously, traveling up to twenty miles a day to find fresh prey and try again.

BENGAL TIGER

The Wildness Inside

In the wild, only the strong survive. For prey animals, this means strong legs for running or strong wings for flying. And for predators, strong limbs for chasing, strong claws for catching, and strong teeth for biting. It is a continuous saga of the hunter and the hunted. Predators and prey alike do not simply live; they survive. And the daily struggle to survive marks the difference between wild and tame, between the well-fed tigers we see up close in a zoo and the ever-hungry tigers encountered in the wild. But make no mistake: Every tame lion, tiger, bear, or wolf is tame only because it is being fed and cared for. Their wildness never dies, but only sleeps inside them. And it is their wildness as well as their beauty that stirs our thoughts as we imagine them with all their power and instinct and all their deadly teeth and lethal claws, unrestrained, uncontained, dangerous, magnificent, living wild and free.

Author's Note

Before I began the paintings for this book, I read a wonderful book about animal art by Bob Kuhn who, in my opinion, is the greatest of all large-mammal painters. His paintings of tigers remain unsurpassed and have always been my favorite Kuhn works. In his book, the artist reveals that he had never seen a tiger in the wild. They were rare during his lifetime. They are still rare today. Every tiger painting he created was based on tigers he observed in zoos. Learning this bolstered my own efforts to paint the pictures in this book, using every resource available to me.

Tooth & Claw is a compilation of many sources. In my life I have been fortunate to have befriended some great wildlife experts. All were natural teachers who generously shared their knowledge with me. Dr. Leonard Lee Rue III routinely mailed me videotapes of the wildlife he was filming in Africa. The footage was "raw" in that it included all the ambient sounds of wind blowing, grass and leaves rustling, animals and birds calling, and even the whispering of the photographer as he was hiding in the bush. Another friend, Jim Brett, answered all my questions about wildlife he has observed on his many travels on the African continent.

For my wife, Deanna, to photograph and for me to see and study the anatomy of the big cats pictured in this book, we traveled to zoos in Illinois, Ohio, Texas, Georgia, and Florida, as well as to a number of state and private preserves. An injured panther being cared for at the Homosassa Springs Wildlife State Park in Florida provided me with good close-up looks at this native cat,

JAGUAR   MOUNTAIN LION

which is so elusive in the wild. A bronze cast of an African lion track I obtained years ago and life sketches I have made over the years of footprints found while tracking bears and mountain lions in the woods and mountains around my home have all added to my understanding of the animals whose portraits I have painted for this book.

We learned a lot about wolves and got to photograph and videotape them at the Lakota Wolf Preserve in Columbia, New Jersey. There, in the state's beautiful northern mountains, with wolves in the forest, it was hard to believe that we were only a few hours' drive from New York City.

We have explored grizzly habitat in Yellowstone, visited red wolf habitat in Texas and South Carolina, and immersed ourselves in panther habitat in the Everglades National Park and Big Cypress National Preserve, both located in southern Florida.

Whenever you find something so interesting you want to draw, paint, write about, or simply study it, use all the resources you can muster. Read books. Search the Internet. And weigh the information from one source against another until you feel you have isolated the truth. Go outdoors and ask people who know about your chosen subject. Above all, let yourself become enthralled. When I am working on a book, I think about it even in my dreams. And every morning I awake to another day of discovery.

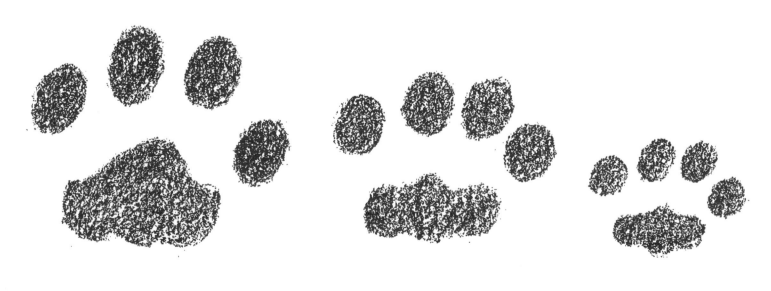

LYNX   BOBCAT   HOUSE CAT

More About Big Carnivores

Arnosky, Jim. *Wild Tracks!: A Guide to Nature's Footprints.*
New York, NY: Sterling Publishing, 2008.

Arnosky, Jim. *Wolves: A One Whole Day Book.* Washington, D.C.:
National Geographic Children's Books, 2001.

Hamilton, S. L. *Xtreme Predators: Bears.* Minneapolis, MN:
ABDO Publishing Company, 2010.

Johns, Chris and Carney, Elizabeth. *Face to Face with Cheetahs.*
Washington, D.C.: National Geographic Children's Books, 2008.

Joubert, Dereck and Joubert, Beverly. *Face to Face with Lions.*
Washington, D.C.: National Geographic Children's Books, 2010.

Lourie, Peter. *The Polar Bear Scientists.* New York, NY: Houghton
Mifflin Books for Children, 2012.

McLeese, Don. *Gray Wolves: Eye to Eye with Endangered Species.*
Vero Beach, FL: Rourke Publishing, 2011.

Read, Tracy C. *Exploring the World of Cougars.* Richmond Hill, ON:
Firefly Books, Ltd., 2011.

Rosing, Norbert. *The World of the Polar Bear.* Richmond Hill, ON:
Firefly Books, Ltd., 2010.

Sartore, Joel. *Face to Face with Grizzlies.* Washington, D.C.:
National Geographic Children's Books, 2009.

Sexton, Colleen. *The Bengal Tiger: Nature's Deadliest.* Minneapolis,
MN: Bellwether Media, 2011.

Simon, Seymour. *Wolves.* New York, NY: HarperCollins, 2009.

Swinburne, Stephen R. *Black Bear: North America's Bear.* Honesdale,
PA: Boyds Mills Press, 2009.

Walker, Sally M. *Jaguars: Nature Watch.* Minneapolis, MN:
Lerner Publications, 2008.

Bear tooth (actual size)

Bear claw (actual size)

Coyote

African lion skull